Credits

Many people have contributed to the completion of this book. For help with locations, I would especially like to thank photographer Jim Schafer in Pittsburgh, photographer Mel Horst in Witmer, Bill West in Philadelphia, and Bill O'Neil in Aliquippa. Also helpful were Chris Umble and Deb Hickok of the Commonwealth of Pennsylvania in Harrisburg, and Donna Albert and John Chepelsky at Ketchum Communications in Pittsburgh. Other people involved were Maria DiBattista in Lancaster County, Benjamin and Lena Lapp in New Holland, and Don Mild in Oil City.

Edited by James B. Patrick and Lindsay Eckford

Designed by Donald G. Paulhus

Printed in Japan

ISBN 0-89909-129-6

First printing 1987

Published by
Foremost Publishers, Inc.
An affiliate of Yankee Publishing Inc.
Dublin, New Hampshire 03444

PENNSYLVANIA

A Scenic Discovery

PHOTOGRAPHY BY ROBERT LLEWELLYN

Introduction by Douglas Day

Published by Foremost Publishers, Inc.
An affiliate of Yankee Publishing Inc.

Overleaf: Bucks County

Introduction

When my friend Robert Llewellyn asked me to write this preface, I was happy to accept, realizing that now I would finally have the opportunity really to learn something about Pennsylvania.

As a schoolboy growing up in Virginia, I thought I knew what Pennsylvania was: a very large rectangle, a little ragged on the Atlantic side, just above the Mason-Dixon Line – and thus for me, a small Confederate, in Enemy Territory. I learned about Betsy Ross, the Liberty Bell, Valley Forge, The Continental Congress, Gettysburg, mighty Pittsburgh; about great rivers with great names: Monongahela, Susquehanna. About Conestoga wagons, Kentucky rifles. About the Johnstown Flood of 1889. (I didn't know it then, but there had already been a second flood, in 1936; and I couldn't have known that there would be yet another one, in 1971: what could there be in Johnstown, I would wonder much later, that would keep its citizens there in the face of such bad luck?) The Keystone State. Gateway to the West. Clearly, there was a lot going on up there in Pennsylvania.

How does one learn about a state that is not one's own? For an American, southern or not, there are the movies. From them I would see images of harsh steel mills and magnificently wild terrain in *The Deer Hunter;* an almost mythical degree of sophistication from Cary Grant and Katharine Hepburn in *The Philadelphia Story;* an almost mythical degree of *un*-sophistication (and another part of Philadelphia entirely) from the *Rocky* series; and a not-altogether specious treatment of the Amish in the recent *Witness.* But all of this exposure did little to give me a coherent sense of what Pennsylvania is, so my curiosity grew. I realize now that my ambitions to circumscribe the state were doomed to failure: not just because it is so large (twenty-six million acres, to be exact) or so diverse (sixty-seven counties, each crying out for its own history and description), but because one no more gets to know a state than one gets to know a person. I would have to be content with allowing fragments of Pennsylvania to drift down into my consciousness however they chose.

At a prep school in Maryland, one which specialized in cramming high school football players from Pennsylvania's coal and steel towns into the Naval Academy, I learned that until then I had not known what toughness was. My friends (thank God they were my friends!) were guys like Duke Wuzzardo and Stan Prahalis, from Scranton and Pottstown respectively. I don't know what ever happened to them, but I hope they're on our side, wherever they are. My first experience with Pennsylvania's labyrinthine ethnic mix was, thus, tinged with a certain sense of potential menace. I was to learn more later about that mix, about the German Moravians, about Slovaks, Hungarians, Croatians, Alsatians, Greeks, Carpatho-Russians, Poles, Blacks, and – most recently – Puerto Ricans, Vietnamese, and Cambodians. Things were simpler for us Blue Ridge Virginians: we were mostly Scots-Irish, with a sprinkling of Welsh and a few Hessians left over from the Revolutionary War. Biologically speaking, our gene pool was infinitely smaller than Pennsylvania's – and not nearly as interesting, culturally speaking.

Still later, as a young Marine Corps second lieutenant, I was hauled from one Civil War battlefield to another, ostensibly to learn tactics and strategy. To go from Virginia's Wilderness Campaign, which was messy and horrifying (men tripped and fell over densely tangled honeysuckle vines, and died in burning forests, never touched by bullets), up to the smooth, rolling hills of Gettysburg, was deceptive. Gettysburg looked easy by comparison. I walked its vast fields, and learned that in a few days in the summer of 1863 more than 50,000 Americans had died there. As I read about one heroic but senseless battle after another, I knew why the South was beaten after that climactic battle. Gettysburg is still, to me, the most instructive place in Pennsylvania.

But it was not until I was a graduate student at the University of Virginia, and began some serious reading about our history, that I began to see that Pennsylvania was at least as important to the making of America as Virginia was. That Thomas Jefferson should have said of William Penn, Pennsylvania's first sole owner and proprietor, that he was "the greatest law-giver the world has produced," was truly striking, since Jefferson was not given to hyperbole. He meant what he said, and I soon learned why.

In the face of severe religious oppression, at a time (between 1660 and 1680) when some 11,000 English Quakers were jailed for their non-conformism, King Charles II gave to his loyal subject William Penn an enormous tract of land in the New World. (It was for some time second only to England herself in size within the commonwealth.) Penn must have been a little like Voltaire's Candide, who thought of living in "a land of happy people, just and kind and bold and free"; for he called his Penn-sylvania-to-be his "faire land," his "holy experiment," a land of freedom open to all who wished to flee from Europe's wars and religious persecutions. History records few successful Utopians, but Penn seems to have been one of them. He himself was able to spend only three years in his Utopia, but in that time he oversaw the founding of dozens of colonies, every member of each one there to find not Candide's El Dorado (though there was plenty of wealth here to be found and pulled from the earth), but something better: freedom. Penn told his settlers that "Ye shall be governed by laws of your own making." And in a document that he called the "Great Law" he wrote that "No person shall be molested or preju-diced for his or her conscientious persuasion or practice. Nor shall he or she at any time be compelled to frequent or maintain any religious wor-ship, place or ministry whatever, contrary to his or her mind. . . . If any person shall abuse or deride any other for his or her different persuasion or practice in matters of religion, such person shall be looked upon as a disturber of the peace and be punished accordingly." (As I first read all of this, I could not help but think of Pennsylvania as a fortunate wedge of benevolence, sandwiched in between the rigid and punitive Pilgrims of New England to the north, and the specter of slavery to the south. Why, Penn treated even the Indians well – which makes him almost unique among founding fathers. And as I read this now, I am struck by Penn's use of "his and her": a man far ahead of his time, clearly.)

Penn needed a capital for his faire land, and he constructed it *ex nihil.*

He had the name already in mind when he first came to the state: Philadelphia, the City of Brotherly Love. (A sect related to the Quakers in England had called themselves Philadelphians, and this caught Penn's fancy.) He found a location on the Delaware River, with beach and harbor. Here he proposed to build a "green country town," a city more pleasant and orderly than those he had known in Europe, or those he saw in the New World, growing up and out any way they chose. His Philadelphia should have no crooked streets; all of them should be ample and spacious, all leading down to the river. He made sure that there would be room for new streets; he specified a commercial district near the river; and he stipulated that all homeowners build their houses in the center of their lots, "so that there may be ground on each side for gardens, orchards or field, that it may be a green country town which will never be burnt and will always be wholesome."

As I say, Penn succeeded. With astonishing rapidity, the oppressed, the diverse, and intransigent minorities like the Quakers poured into the state. By the mid-1700s, no city in the Empire — except for London — had more English-speakers than Philadelphia. (One ought to note here, though, that in the eighteenth century almost as many Pennsylvanians spoke German as English: the result of the great influx of Anabaptists — Moravians, Mennonites, Amish, and Pietists — into Penn's Commonwealth.)

What Penn began so brilliantly, Benjamin Franklin solidified. Under the guidance of Franklin, Philadelphia became the country's intellectual center, with his American Philosophical Society and his University of Pennsylvania as its core. (For reasons of family pride, I'll note here that my great-grandfather did his medical internship at Penn in 1852; and that my son is there now, working on his doctorate in Folklore.) William Penn is a little elusive, a little ethereal, in Pennsylvania today; but Franklin is everywhere as a real presence, not only in the statues one sees of him, but in the sense of busy pragmatism that one feels throughout the state: a very effective counterbalance to Penn's Utopianism. Whatever else he might have been, Franklin was the embodiment of the notion that hard work must surely be rewarded. We love him for his *Poor Richard's Almanack;* but we often forget that behind it was a man who could write of his almanack that "I reaped considerable profit from it, vending annually nearly ten thousand." Among the state's illustrious sons, the Quaker George Fox might seem most to follow Penn; but beside every Fox there is an Andrew Carnegie, a man who must have memorized all of Poor Richard's aphorisms. Pennsylvania (and the whole country) has benefited equally from both lines of descent.

In all this historical summary, I suspect I am preaching to the already converted. Even Southerners and Bostonians (and maybe even New Yorkers) will admit that Philadelphia is the cradle of the nation's intellect. What interests me more about the city is its amazing ethnic diversity: wherever I went this past fall I saw Korean Catholic churches, Ethiopian cafés, Thai restaurants — you name it (and around the next corner there'll be something you don't even know how to begin to name). But in all this welter of ethnicity, one does not feel threatened, alienated. Another legacy of Penn: these people are here to live their lives, to be let alone, and to leave others alone.

There is no time to speak of the physical beauty of Pennsylvania. I'll let Robert Llewellyn's photographs do that for me. Nor can I speak of Pittsburgh's amazing rejuvenation and vitality; nor of the state's western half, that wilder part cut off from the east by the diagonal slash of the Appalachians. Nor of the Poconos, nor Bucks County, nor of the Grand Canyon in the north-center of the state, with its thousand-foot gorges and its white-water rapids. To have to deal so briefly with Pennsylvania is frustrating. What *must* be said, though, is that three-fifths of the state is still forest: a most felicitous blend of southern and northern hardwoods, with more wildflowers than I could begin to name. White-tail deer are everywhere. The rivers are full of trout. The only word that suits here is plenitude, God's bounty.

Nowhere is this bounty more obvious than in Lancaster County, in the southeastern section of the state. Here is the home of the Amish, they of the Gentle Persuasion. There are more than 6000 farms in Lancaster County, and most of them are owned and worked by the Amish and their not-so-strict cousins, the Mennonites.

One can observe the Amish, but not much more. They do not relish conversations with outsiders. At home and with one another they speak an evolved form of German that we call "Pennsylvania Dutch"; English is their second language. Their adults generally refuse to be photographed, lest their parishes accuse them of vanity. They keep to themselves, run their own schools (which end with the eighth grade), make their own severely simple clothes, marry among themselves, will go neither to war nor to court. They ride everywhere in their black buggies drawn by well-groomed horses. Where they must use something modern – like plows and harrows, or electric milking machines – they do so with reluctance. Their farms are the most prosperous and productive in the country: partly because of the county's rich, black soil, but chiefly because of their dogged, tenacious industriousness – and their shrewdness: they are canny people, these Amish. Candide would love them, but they wouldn't take him in. Too scatterbrained, they'd say.

Henry Adams wrote of the Pennsylvania of 1800 that it was "the only true democratic community . . . the ideal American state, easy, tolerant, and contented." Not even the most chauvinistic Pennsylvanian would claim that Adams' praise would fit the state today. Perfection is as hard to hold on to as it is to attain. But I, an outsider, will say that Pennsylvania still seems a *possible* place, a place where one can imagine himself living well and happily. It's hard to define, but there's a *solidity* to Pennsylvania that makes one want to say that, if he were required to define what was American about America, he would start with a description of Pennsylvania.

Douglas Day

Hyner View, Clinton County

Cambria County

Old Bedford Village, Bedford County

Hopewell Village, Montgomery County

Longwood Gardens, Chester County

Hershey Gardens, Dauphin

Overleaf: Cook Forest, Clarion County

Covered Bridge, Bedford County

Cauliflower Harvest, Lancaster County

Heinz Hall, Pittsburgh Cathedral of Learning, University of Pittsburgh

Mummers Parade, Philadelphia

Mummers Parade, Philadelphia

Hopewell Village, Montgomery County

Amish Schoolgirl, Lancaster County

Covered Bridge, Lancaster County

Longwood Gardens, Chester County

Longwood Gardens, Chester County

Hopewell Village, Montgomery County

Dickinson College, Carlisle, Cumberland County   *Overleaf:* Hyner View, Clinton County

Amish Schoolhouse, Lancaster County

Washington Crossing, Bucks County

State Capitol Building, Harrisburg

Business District, Pittsburgh

Overleaf: Fly fishing, Wayne County

Ricketts Glen, Luzerne County

Allegheny National Forest, Forest County   Allegheny National Forest, Elk County

Hopewell Village, Montgomery County

Brandywine Battlefield, Chester County

Grand Canyon of Pennsylvania, Tioga County   Lake Erie County

Presque Isle, Erie County

Presque Isle, Erie County

Devon Horse Show, Chester County

Devon Horse Show, Chester County

Franklin Institute, Philadelphia

Cliveden, Germantown, Philadelphia

Overleaf: Pittsburgh

Assembly Room, Independence Hall, Philadelphia   Benjamin Franklin Parkway, Philadelphia

Ukrainian Catholic Church, Pittsburgh

Independence Hall, Philadelphia

Liberty Bell, Philadelphia   *Overleaf:* McConnell's Mill, Lawrence County

PPG Tower, Pittsburgh

Plaza, PPG Place, Pittsburgh

Chambersburg, Franklin County

Frank Lloyd Wright's "Falling Water," Fayette County

McConnell's Mill, Lawrence County   *Overleaf:* Lighthouse, Presque Isle, Erie County

Susquehanna River, Harrisburg

Society Hill, Philadelphia

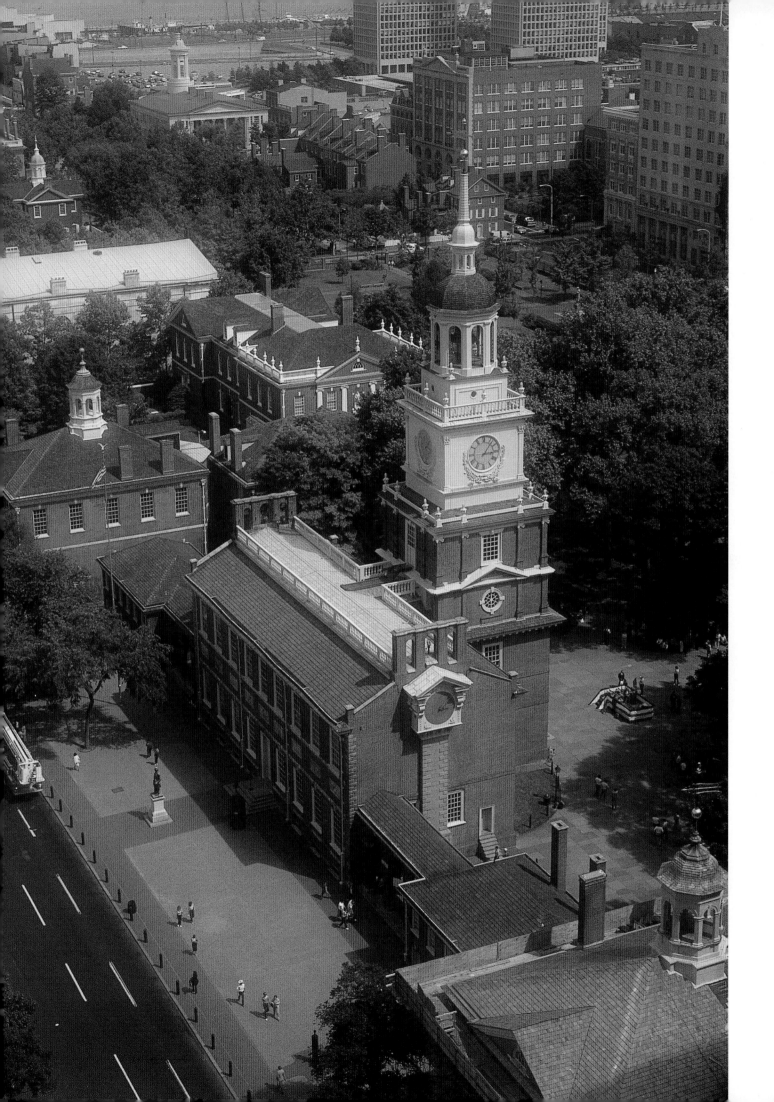

Independence Hall, Philadelphia

University of Pennsylvania, Philadelphia

Near Doe Run, Chester County

Bucks County

Overleaf: Lancaster County

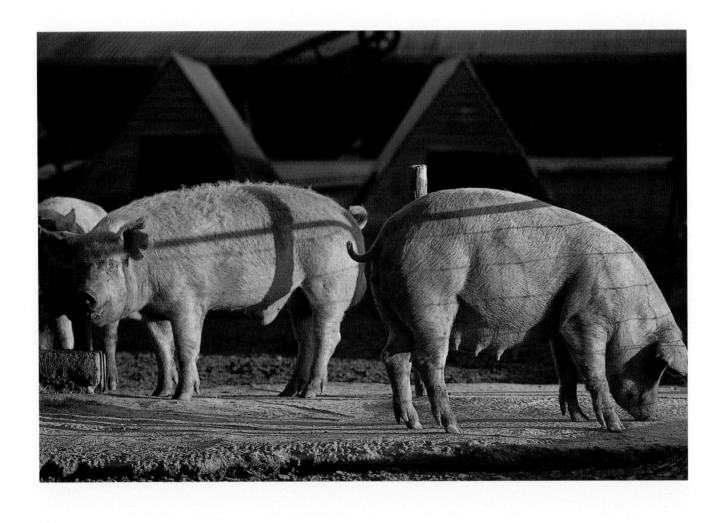

Franklin County

Central Market, Lancaster

Bedford County

Quakertown, Bucks County

Cook Forest, Clarion County

Drake Well Museum, Venango County   *Overleaf:* Grand Canyon of Pennsylvania, Tioga County

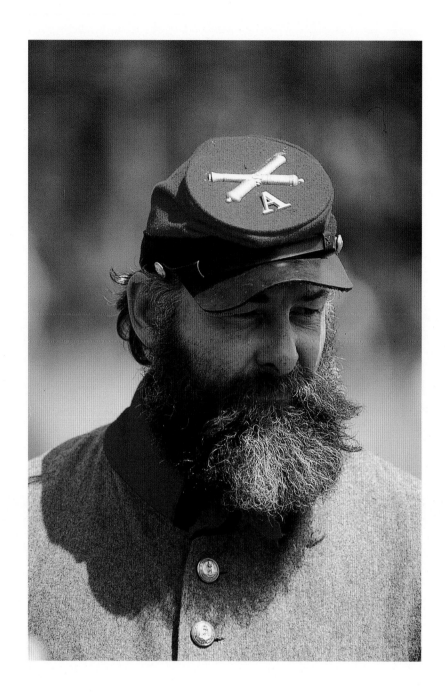

Civil War Reenactment, Gettysburg, Adams County

Pennsylvania War Memorial, Gettysburg Battlefield, Adams County

Civil War Reenactment, Gettysburg Battlefield, Adams County

Washington Crossing, Bucks County

Battle of Germantown Reenactment, Philadelphia

Battle of Germantown Reenactment, Philadelphia

Overleaf: Bedford County

Washington Crossing, Bucks County

Washington Crossing, Bucks County

Hopewell Village, Montgomery County

Strasburg Railroad, Lancaster County

Ohiopyle State Park, Fayette County

Overleaf: Somerset County

Winter encampment, Valley Forge, Montgomery County

Valley Forge, Montgomery County

Corn Harvest, Lancaster County

Corn Crib, Bedford County

Fayette County

Mushroom Farm, Chester County